Know The Way,
Keep The Truth,
Win The Life

Know The Way, Keep The Truth, Win The Life

DONALD MACLEOD

SERMONS FOR THE MIDDLE THIRD OF THE PENTECOST SEASON

(SUNDAYS IN ORDINARY TIME)

CYCLE B GOSPEL TEXTS

C.S.S. Publishing Co., Inc.

Lima, Ohio

KNOW THE WAY, KEEP THE TRUTH. . .

Library of Congress Cataloging-in-Publication Data

Macleod, Donald, 1913-
    Know the way, keep the truth, win the life.

    (Cycle B gospel texts)
    1. Church year sermons.   2. Bible. N.T. Gospels —
Sermons.   3. Sermons, American.   I. Title.   II. Series.
BV4253.M375   1987   252'.6   87-10303
ISBN 0-89536-872-2

7858 / ISBN 0-89536-872-2   PRINTED IN U.S.A.

Table of Contents

[1] Common Lectionary
[2] Lutheran Lectionary
[3] Roman Catholic Lectionary

Lectionary Preaching After Pentecost

Virtually all pastors who make use of the sermons in this book will find their worship life and planning shaped by one of two lectionary series. Most mainline Protestant denominations, along with clergy of the Roman Catholic Church, have now approved — either for provisional or official use — the three-year Common (Consensus) Lectionary. This family of denominations includes United Methodist, Presbyterian, United Church of Christ, and Disciples of Christ.

Lutherans and Roman Catholics, while testing the Common Lectionary on a limited basis at present, follow their own three-year cycle of texts. While there are divergences between the Common and Lutheran/Roman Catholic systems, the gospel texts show striking parallels, with few text selections evidencing significant differences. Virtually all the gospel texts included in this book will, therefore, be applicable to worship and preaching planning for clergy following either lectionary.

A significant divergence does occur, however, in the method by which specific gospel texts are assigned to specific calendar days. The Common and Roman Catholic lectionaries accomplish this by counting backwards from Christ the King (Last Sunday after Pentecost), discarding "extra" texts from the front of the list; Lutherans follow the opposite pattern, counting forward from The Holy Trinity, discarding "extra" texts at the end of the list.

The following index will aid the user of this book in matching the right text to the right Sunday during the "Pentecost Half" of the church year (days listed here include only those appropriate to this book's contents):

Fixed Date Lectionaries   **Lutheran Lectionary**

Text Designation

Common	*Roman Catholic*	
Proper 12 *July 24-30*	Ordinary Time 17	Pentecost 10
Proper 13 *July 31 — August 6*	Ordinary Time 18	Pentecost 11
Proper 14 *August 7-13*	Ordinary Time 19	Pentecost 12

Fixed-date Lectionaries		Lutheran Lectionary
Common	*Roman Catholic*	
Proper 15 *August 14-20*	Ordinary Time 20	Pentecost 13
Proper 16 *August 21-27*	Ordinary Time 21	Pentecost 14
Proper 17 *August 28 — September 3*	Ordinary Time 22	Pentecost 15
Proper 18 *September 4-10*	Ordinary Time 23	Pentecost 16
Proper 19 *September 11-17*	Ordinary Time 24	Pentecost 17
Proper 20 *September 18-24*	Ordinary Time 25	Pentecost 18
Proper 21 *September 25 — October 1*	Ordinary Time 26	Penteocst 19
Proper 22 *October 2-8*	Ordinary Time 27	Pentecost 20

First Series

Up-Dating Out-Dated "Holy"

After this Jesus went to the other side of the Sea of Galilee, which is the Sea of Tiberias. And a multitude followed him, because they saw the signs which he did on those who were diseased. Jesus went up on the mountain, and there sat down with his disciples. Now the Passover, the feast of the Jews, was at hand. Lifting up his eyes, then, and seeing that a multitude was coming to him, Jesus said to Philip, "How are we to buy bread, so that these people may eat?" This he said to test him, for he himself knew what he would do. Philip answered him, "Two hundred denarii would not buy enough bread for each of them to get a little." One of his disciples, Andrew, Simon Peter's brother, said to him, "There is a lad here who had five barley loaves and two fish; but what are they among so many?" Jesus said, "Make the people sit down." Now there was much grass in the place; so the men sat down, in number about five thousand. Jesus then took the loaves, and when he had given thanks, he distributed them to those who were seated; so also the fish, as much as they wanted. And when they had eaten their fill, he told his disciples, "Gather up the fragments left over, that nothing may be lost." So they gathered them up and filled twelve baskets with fragments from the five barley loaves, left by those who had eaten. When the people saw the sign which he had done, they said, "This is indeed the prophet who is to come into the world!"

Perceiving then that they were about to come and take him by force to make him king, Jesus withdrew again to the mountain by himself.

John 6:1-15 (RSV)

John 6:1-15

Holy Arithmetic

"There is a lad here. . ." (v. 9)

Basic education in America has been labeled the "3 R's," from the homespun rhyme:
  "Reading, and 'Riting, and 'Rithmetic
  Taught to the tune of a hickory stick."
Arithmetic, however, had four main foci: addition, subtraction, division, and multiplication. The Bible uses all four of these in matters of faith and belief, but the paramount one is *"multiply."*

Our text comes from the well-known New Testament story of Jesus' feeding of the five thousand. Reflect for a moment on the situation the writer, John, presents here. It is a picture of Jesus' amazing popularity. But it had its price. As one commentator wrote: "He was hedged around with eyes — kindly or critical, adoring or questioning, reverent or cynical. They all watched him." And this occasion was no exception. He and his disciples had gone to the other side of the Sea of Galilee, in all likelihood an effort to escape, but the crowd followed him and had now swelled into the thousands. Furthermore, these people were now so hungry that the situation developed quickly into an emergency. Where and how could food be secured for this teeming crowd? The disciples were empty-handed. They had no supplies or resources. They seemed helpless. Moreover, there was no money. Philip aggravated the situation by saying, despairingly, that it would take more than six month's wages to feed a throng such as this. And Andrew, as if snatching at a straw, remarked as a seeming understatement, "There is a lad here who has five barley loaves and two fish. . ."

On the surface, it appeared as a ridiculous fact, but it was the turning point in the desperate situation. It was Jesus' opportunity to put one of his external principles to work — in one word: multiply. Nothing was to be added, subtracted, or divided — all was to be multiplied — and the fragments filled twelve baskets (v. 13). Maybe it was a miracle. Maybe it was John's allegorizing an overture of faith. But, all in all, it is a telling illustration of what Jesus can do with the smallest capacity of human belief or the most meager talent you or I possess. Never was his strategy a matter of merely addition — attempting to satisfy us by giving us more and more bread. Nor was it by subtraction — he aimed to fulfill the Law, not lop pieces off it. Nor did he favor dividing people into religious levels, as did the Pharisees — all persons, to him, were equally in need of redemption. He called everyone to spiritual commitment to God's will, so that their talents, gifts, and capacities could be multiplied. J. Ithel Jones of Cardiff declared, "Little is much when God is in it." It is not how much we have, but what is done with what we have. Once Jesus said, "According to your faith be it unto you."

The Bible has its many examples. Moses is called by God, but he protests, "I am not eloquent . . ." God, however, counteracts, "Go, I will be with you." Jeremiah is tapped by God, but he shouts back, "Behold, I cannot speak, for I am a child. . ." God contradicts him, "Be not afraid of their face; for I am with you." In these and every similar case, God took the minimal and multiplied it by his own omnipotence. F. W. Norwood, the Australian preacher, observed: "Every notable name in our own history is a name that confounded arithmetic." And Dwight L. Moody remarked: "The world has yet to see what God can do with and for and by a person that is wholly consecrated to him." All these put what they had in the hands of God and he multiplied their gift. "There is a lad here. . ."

1. For us in our day, there lies here, first of all, the secret of our redemption. God takes, we said, what we can offer and when we invest our faith in its use, he multiplies it. Maybe it is a spare hour given by a busy businessman to teach a Sunday school class every week. Maybe it is a brief moment taken by a harried mother to teach her children their evening prayers. Maybe it is a few hours given by a university student every weekend to coach a team of orphaned boys whose daily horizon is a slum. These are merely fragments, scattered pieces of humanity, but in the hands of such dedicated persons, the possibilities of human hearts are multiplied. Jesus said of the woman who anointed his head, "She did what she could." Someone may raise a caveat and ask what do these simple deeds achieve in the face of the demoralizing forces on every hand today — pornography, risque films, drugs, narcotics, and the whole smear? "There is a lad here with five barley loaves and two fish." (Barley bread was the cheapest kind and considered fit only for animals in those days; and, to be edible after hours under the hot sun, the rest of the snack had to be pickled fish.) But, in the hands of Jesus, these and our own simple gifts can be multiplied one hundredfold, to save from spiritual starvation the needy throngs of this earth. Cawley of Trinidad said, decades ago: "The difference between worth and worthlessness is the Master's blessing." Jesus says of what we have and are, "Bring them to me." These are ours to give him. He will multiply them by his power.

2. Here lies also the secret of the church's expansion. Talk about the church these days resolves itself very frequently in terms of the wrong sectors of arithmetic. Statistics occupy our plans and reports: members gained or lost; deficits deplored and percentage advances celebrated; attendance records up and

down; and status in the community measured with satisfaction or concern. This is the wrong arithmetic! The church, its witness and outreach, its mission to humankind, does not belong in the maze of pluses and minuses. Someone needs to declare, "There is a lad here. . ." In the world of nature, a seed does not add or subtract or divide; it multiplies. The secret of expansion is to take what we have, nourish it with the living elixir of the Gospel, and allow it to grow into spiritual maturity.

3. Further, here lies the secret of our spiritual stamina. Note v. 15: "When Jesus perceived they were about to take him by force and make him a king, he withdrew again to the hills by himself." His ministry was besieged increasingly now by the crowds. His private life was shrinking. The needy, the curious (Nicodemus, for example), the concerned beleaguered him by day and night. The crowds, however, wanted to add (revive the lost glories of Israel); subtract (smash Rome); divide (carve out a new Jewish empire); but Jesus wanted to plant, in each soul, the seedling of God's kingdom and, by holy living, i.e., repentance, prayer, and faith, allow it to multiply, until a new age of love and peace would claim the allegiance of the inhabited earth.

To maintain this vision and purpose, Jesus needed spiritual reserves, not military or political power. The people wanted to make him a king, but, John said, "He withdrew again to the hills by himself." He could not simply give to them what they needed without drawing upon spiritual reserves as necessary for himself. In those solitary hours, alone in communion with God, he gained perspective, resources, and stamina wherewith to go on.

And so with us. The work of the kingdom, inside and outside the church, is often misrepresented and foiled by contrary notions of masses of people who want their own ends and their own way. All of us should heed the voice in the crowd saying, "There is a lad here . . .," meaning, "O living Savior, we do not need strength to do what *we* want to do; we need stamina from you to multiply the little we have, to fulfill what *you* want us to do."

16

So when the people saw that Jesus was not there, nor his disciples, they themselves got into the boats and went to Capernaum, seeking Jesus.

When they found him on the other side of the sea, they said to him, "Rabbi, when did you come here?" Jesus answered them, "Truly, truly, I say to you, you seek me, not because you saw signs, but because you ate your fill of the loaves. Do not labor for the food which perishes, but for the food which endures to eternal life, which the Son of man will give to you; for on him has God the Father set his seal." Then they said to him, "What must we do, to be doing the works of God?" Jesus answered them, "This is the work of God, that you believe in him whom he has sent." So they said to him, "Then what sign do you do, that we may see, and believe you? What work do you perform? Our fathers ate the manna in the wilderness; as it is written, 'He gave them bread from heaven to eat.' " Jesus then said to them, "Truly, truly, I say to you, it was not Moses who gave you the bread from heaven; my Father gives you the true bread from heaven. For the bread of God is that which comes down from heaven, and gives life to the world." They said to him, "Lord, give us this bread always."

Jesus said to them, "I am the bread of life; he who comes to me shall not hunger, and he who believes in me shall never thirst.

John 6:24-35 (RSV)

John 6:24-35

Holy Diet

Jesus said to them, "I am the bread of life; he who comes to me shall not hunger, and he who believes in me shall never thirst." (v. 35)

In a broadcast address in London, T. S. Eliot talked about "spiritual awareness." He observed that many persons aspire to become Christians and believe, presumably, in the efficacy of the Christian faith, but never reach the stage of actually experiencing it. Aspiring towards real belief, i.e., becoming truly Christian, is one thing, whereas complete awareness of it is another. Aspiring can easily become an end in itself. And, as Charles H. Duthie of Edinburgh remarked: "It is a matter of living forever in the preface and never becoming involved in the story."

This condition of spiritual awareness is clearly defined by Jesus in the words of our text. It is a state of soul devoutly and eagerly to be aspired to, in contrast to what Lord Cecil of Britain once referred to as "believing in God in a common-place sort of way." And, it becomes the gift and possession of any persons who are utterly dissatisfied with themselves, and who decide to fulfill those important requisites that make them completely satisfied in Christ.

What were the circumstances that drew this strong and telling remark from Jesus? It was the morning after the day he had fed the five thousand on the Galilean hillside. He and the disciples had crossed the lake, but the people followed them. Uppermost in their thinking was the human cry for bread. Moreover, behind it all was their misconception of Jesus' mission and their notion that life was a matter of performing certain things, in order to qualify to receive what they wanted. Jesus undertook now to set them straight. For him, life was a matter of being, not merely of doing. By so saying, he sorted out for them their priorities: ordinary bread that feeds and satisfies the body can be earned, but the bread Jesus offered them had to do with the inner life; it comes as a gift to those whose spiritual lifestyle qualifies them to receive it. Hence their question, "What must we *do*?" (v. 28) was out of order. Bread for mind and soul asks more accurately, "What must we *be*?"

At this point, Jesus did not leave them confused or in the dark over the nature of his mission and purpose among them. Their motives were worldly; his, moral and spiritual. They were materially ambitious and they had hoped to have found, in Jesus, a potential political leader who would restore their lost national status and root out the tentacles of Rome. Moreover, the miracle on the hillside was a reason for speculation that maybe an era of free handouts was, for them, just around the corner. But Jesus put the issues into another context entirely. Bread and water were the basic staples of their daily diet, but this man declared, "I am the bread of life. I am the water of life." He offered them himself. "I am the bread of life; he who comes to me shall not hunger, and he who believes in me shall never thirst." What they wanted was not what they needed. The latter was there in their midst; not something to be earned, but received. As St. Augustine wrote: "We do not come to Christ by running or walking, but by believing, not by the motion of the body, but by the will of the mind."

I

There are lessons here for every one of us who aspires towards a level of life where a sense of spiritual awareness holds us fast. "I am the bread of life; he who comes to me shall not hunger." Jesus is instructing us here, first of all, about the true nature of life. Note how the word "life" dominates these lines. And Jesus zeroed in that day upon the attention and interest of the crowd by singling out the two elements that meant most to life — bread and water. These they would think of naturally when the words "life" and "hunger" were mentioned. But Jesus was leading their thinking towards a deeper hunger, for which he himself was the answer and the cure.

Remember, for example, the Prodigal. He had a hunger for independence, the thrill and excitement of living high and fast and wild, entirely free from the dull routine of the farm. But, all too soon, this superficial bread and water, the thrills and frills of sensuous living, reduced him to the level of scrounging for any available scraps of leftover food and drink. Suddenly he came to himself and was arrested by a deeper hunger, a longing for home, family, and love; these were elements without which his soul was starved. Lasting satisfaction began to emerge when, as Luke tells us, "He was a great way off, his father saw him. . ."

Ours is a generation with its own various kinds of hunger. We may deplore, but yet enjoy, what Wordsworth called "this unaimed prattle flying up and down." We may question the American dream, yet acclaim anyone who is "on the make" and aggressively acquiring more and more things. We may take overweening pride in the products of American science and know-how, but we dodge the arresting question: "What's it all for?" Jesus heard the people ask, "Give us this bread always" (v. 34), which today would be put, "Give us everything we want; forget any thought of what we need." This would not be living, and surely it cannot produce true life. "He who comes to me shall not hunger," said Jesus. Why? Because Jesus brings us real bread that can make the poorest life among us an awareness of a great satisfaction. To those who come to him, he gives new moral and spiritual standing (Mark Rutherford spelled out another Beatitude: "Blessed are they who give us back our self-respect"); a new start when the old lifestyle led us downward and got us nowhere; a new character that shook off our self-centeredness and showed us how to use life

in a new way; and a new set of promises to nourish our souls
and give us reason to go on with courage toward innumerable
victories. These are the answers he gives when you and I pray
constantly and sincerely, "Give us this day our daily bread."

II

"He who comes to me" is a somewhat general invitation,
but the matter becomes specific when Jesus added in effect,
"He who comes *believing*. . ." There's the rub. Jesus indicates, in the second place, the manner of being which nour-
ishes and feeds the true life. There are actually two kinds of
bread: material — helps us from without inwards; and spiritual
— helps us from within outwards. Jesus' concern was for the
latter, because the inward life was, to him, the true life. As
one commentator has written: "There is a vacuum in the soul
of man which nothing can fill save faith in God." "He who
believes in me shall never thirst" — shall never be unsatisfied;
shall never lack that chief ingredient needed to provide full
life. Few of us take this seriously. If our physical condition
is not up to par, we run to the physician. If we are frustrated,
despondent, filled with a sense of failure, aimlessness, and lost
meaning, we rarely get upset by it. We long for peace of mind,
fulfillment, and a well-rounded life. We aspire, but fall short
of spiritual awareness. This means: get to know him (read and
reread the Gospels); live with him (talk to him in your prayers); love him (give him the edge of your affection over the
things you crave for and want); and let his presence daily
permeate your whole lifestyle. That is a tall order. It is a holy
diet. It produces moving examples of eternal life.

> *I heard the voice of Jesus say,*
> *"Behold, I freely give*
> *The living water, thirsty one;*
> *Stoop down, and drink, and live."*
> *I came to Jesus, and I drank*
> *Of that life-giving stream;*
> *My thirst was quenched, my soul revived,*
> *And now I live in him.*
>
> — *Horatius Bonar*

Jesus said to them, "I am the bread of life; he who comes to me shall not hunger, and he who believes in me shall never thirst.

The Jews then murmured at him, because he said, "I am the bread which came down from heaven." They said, "Is not this Jesus, the son of Joseph, whose father and mother we know? How does he now say, 'I have come down from heaven'?" Jesus answered them, "Do not murmur among yourselves. No one can come to me unless the Father who sent me draws him; and I will raise him up at the last day. It is written in the prophets, 'And they shall all be taught by God.' Every one who has heard and learned from the Father comes to me. Not that any one has seen the Father except him who is from God; he has seen the Father. Truly, truly, I say to you, he who believes has eternal life. I am the bread of life. your fathers ate the manna in the wilderness, and they died. This is the bread which comes down from heaven, that a man may eat of it and not die. I am the living bread which came down from heaven; if any one eats of this bread, he will live for ever; and the bread which I shall give for the life of the world is my flesh."

John 6:35, 41-51 (RSV)

Holy Believing

"Truly, truly, I say to you, he who believes has eternal life."
(v. 47)

No one wants to die. Yet, who among us would like to live forever? This is our paradox. This is our dilemma. To die means the end of what we are and have; it signifies also the cessation of whatever yet we had hoped to be. But wouldn't living forever be equally undesireable? For it holds out endlessness and sameness, like Shakespeare's "Tomorrow and tomorrow and tomorrow. . ." Such would not be much even of a respite from sheer nothingness. On the other hand, however, who would want to play a harp throughout all time, or listen endlessly to "The Hallelujah Chorus"?

It is obvious, on second thought, that such questions and thinking are colored and even determined by our worldly concepts. Our idioms come from the vocabulary of time and space, and borrow pictures from the poetry of the ages. Maybe such cannot be avoided for good or for ill, nor can our dialogue about religion be completely free from it. What is needed, therefore, is serious caution and concern about the human frame of mind and heart behind it.

Jesus was aware of this when he attempted to teach a mixed gathering of curious folk, whose thinking about his mission and his person was entwined with strains and threads of nationalism, ambition, religious prejudice, and downright spiritual immaturity. Note the verbs in their questions: "What must we *do*, to be doing the work of God?" (v. 28); "Lord, *give* us this bread always" (v. 34); and "The Jews *murmured* at him" (v. 41). There were the activists among them for whom any alliance with God was a matter of "doing." There were also the takers for whom religion meant *give me*, i.e., welfare checks, adequate and regular. Then there were the murmurers, whose religion existed and was exercised in one dimension only and featured no fusion between the earthly and the heavenly.

Now Jesus cut straight across these confused and confusing perspectives and declared, "He who believes has eternal life." Should he say this today to our generation, what would we understand by it? Would it satisfy us who, in our own day, bring notions before the bar of the Christian faith that are equally perplexed and confused? "He who believes" — believes what? Or whom? "Eternal life" — what meaning can the average person put into this phrase today? "Live forever" — did Jesus mean endless existence or life on the deepest level now? Or both? All these seem like separate questions, but they belong really together and the answers can be instruction in our Christian faith.

I

It is important to note how the word *believe* is so crucial and critical in any New Testament discussion about life, especially eternal life. Modern folk, however, raise a red flag and say: "Yes, we yearn for a better life, but beliefs are so many and varied that we do not know where to start." Do not think for one moment that these Jews were in any better situation with their ancient Law and its 613 separate regulations. For us the first step must be: *to believe Jesus*. To believe *in* Jesus raises a score of questions — who he was, what about his strange power, what he meant by giving himself to men and women as bread to eat, and what would be the situation after he had gone. To believe Jesus, however, is to accept him as a person, not this or that about him, but in his totality. After all, Peter, James, John, and Andrew, we read, simply quit their jobs and followed him. Then they went on to accept his word, observe his teachings in action, and come to grips with the truth he declared.

To believe Jesus is living as if what he said about God is true, the good life in the long run spells victory, our human nature has a potential which God alone can bring to fruition, and the lifestyle described in the Sermon on the Mount is the only one that satisfies.

Anyone who has doubts here must remember that Jesus underwrote all this with his own life. He never flinched, even from the Cross. He was indeed the bread of life; and all who would partake of it, i.e., all who believe Jesus and appropriate his person into their life, should discover they have acquired a quality of living which is never lost. It pours its essence into every community and in the ongoing destiny of the human race. This is not a matter of space and time; it is the world of our everyday experience being infused and absorbed by the world of eternity. Doubt it if you will, but to believe Jesus is to hearken to his words to his own disciples: "If it were not so, I would have told you." (John 14:2)

II

A further step: believe Jesus and let his person operate within your life. When you and I consume bread and allow it to go through our digestive processes, its nutrients nourish and strengthen our whole body system so that we can work, think, and aspire as human beings. Jesus claimed to be the Bread of Life. His life, if accepted and received by us, would provide what is necessary for our souls. Paul experienced this working of the person of Christ within his own life when he wrote: ". . .I live; yet not I, but Christ lives in me; and the life I now live in the flesh I live by faith in the Son of God, who loved me and gave himself for me." (Galatians 2:20)

All this, of course, involves commitment to Christ's person. In so doing, you and I ally ourselves (a) with one who is willing and ready to involve himself in the struggle of life with us; and (b) with a purpose which appeared alive in him, and the ends and aims of which are good. We are not on our own; that gets us nowhere. God's intention for all of us is the abundant life and, in Christ, he has shown us the way to it. We need not strain or struggle or force the issue; all we need to do is to ask

Bread of heaven, bread of heaven,
Feed me till I want no more.

To believe Jesus opens up a new relationship with God. This is *the* life. As William Barclay wrote: "Jesus is the essential without which real life can neither begin nor go on." It is a satisfactory way to live here and now. And it bears a glimmering promise that this life with its love, its faith, and its will to become more and more, will never die.

"I am the living bread which came down from heaven; if any one eats of this bread, he will live for ever; and the bread which I shall give for the life of the world is my flesh."

The Jews then disputed among themselves, saying, "How can this man give us his flesh to eat?" So Jesus said to them, "Truly, truly, I say to you, unless you eat the flesh of the Son of man and drink his blood, you have no life in you; he who eats my flesh and drinks my blood has eternal life, and I will raise him up at the last day. For my flesh is food indeed, and my blood is drink indeed. He who eats my flesh and drinks my blood abides in me, and I in him. As the living Father sent me, and I live because of the Father, so he who eats me will live because of me. This is the bread which came down from heaven, not such as the fathers ate and died; he who eats this bread will live for ever." This he said in the synagogue, as he taught at Capernaum.

Many of his disciples, when they heard it, said, "This is a hard saying; who can listen to it?" But Jesus, knowing in himself that his disciples murmured at it, said to them, "Do you take offense at this? Then what if you were to see the Son of man ascending where he was before? It is the spirit that gives life, the flesh is of no avail; the words that I have spoken to you are spirit and life. But there are some of you that do not believe." For Jesus knew from the first who those were that did not believe, and who it was that would betray him. And he said, "This is why I told you that no one can come to me unless it is granted him by the Father."

John 6:51-65 (RSV)

[Author's note: The framers of the three lectionaries served by this book failed to see that John, chapter 6, cannot be broken up into the many pericopes they have designated. Verses 41-51, for example, are exactly the same in substance as v. 51-58; no preacher can produce two different sermons on these passages separately. Hence the more appropriate strategy is to specify the pericope as v. 51-65 — D. M.]

John 6:51-65

Holy Living

"The words that I have spoken to you are spirit and life."
(v. 63b)

Years ago, Harry Emerson Fosdick, then at the height of his influence as minister of the Riverside Church, New York City, was making a tour of Palestine and other countries of the Near and Middle East. He was invited to give an address at the American University of Beirut, Lebanon, where the student body comprised citizens of many countries and representatives from sixteen different religions. What could one say that would be relevant or of interest to so mixed and varied a group? This is how Fosdick began: "I do not ask anyone here to change his religion; but I do ask all of you to face up to this question: What is your religion doing to your character?"

This was a call to consider one of the great issues of human belief: religion and life, Christianity and character, word and spirit. Emerson once said, "What you are speaks so loudly I cannot hear a word you say." Jesus' discourse in this whole sixth chapter of the Gospel of John had two foci — spirit and life. "The words that I have spoken to you are spirit and life." By this he meant that those who appropriated his spirit, i.e., fed upon him as the bread of life, would find, thereby, a fulfillment and satisfaction no other means could give.

The traditions of the world of his time, of course, had a different emphasis. The Greeks were in search of a formula for life, a slogan by which to perform, but such could never claim the commitment of the human will. The Jews had their Law, demanding obedience to every detail as the requisite to the good life, but St. Paul discovered that a set of rules could never provide salvation nor solve the deadly problem of sin and moral failure. Jesus, however, came with a new key to true life: accept his spirit, surrender to the claim of his will, allow him to enter the stream of everyday living; and, in this commitment, all we say and do will reflect the influence of his life within us.

What does this do for and with those who resolve to do it? How has it worked in the Christian story?

1. The world saw the effect of this new spirit in the early church. When these early followers of Jesus fanned out into the Mediterranean world, they brought with their Christianity something the pagan world lacked and sorely needed. The spirit of hope and expectation, for example, had become snuffed out and a sense of defeat, meaninglessness, and fascination with the bizarre settled down upon their thinkers and philosophers. As J. Robert Seeley wrote, "Philosophy could explain what is right, but only Christianity could help people to do it." Whatever may have been uncouth and unimpressive about these early Christians, it was always forgotten when people saw the radiant light on their faces. And no pagan philosopher had ever seen anything quite like it — a religion so identified with life that it transformed human personalities and filled their lives with direction, meaning, and high expectation. They seemed to be nourished and empowered by something outside and beyond themselves; with this possession, they made a disturbing impact upon the ancient world.

2. The world saw the effect of this new spirit upon human conduct. Ian Macpherson explained this when he wrote: "When Jesus takes possession of the heart, everything else is

changed." Someone once said, "Despair has three heads: agnosticism, which makes us lose courage in our search for knowledge; pessimism, which makes us lose courage in our search for progress; and cynicism, which makes us lose courage in our search for virtue." If there is any disease rampant in our common life today it is cynicism. And one of the favorite questions it asks is: "What difference does it make what one believes?" But those who are so ready to ask this question fail to see that it is followed logically and inevitably by another — "Does it make any difference what a person does?" And the answer one gives to this second question determines the answer one should give to the first. For the cynic, everything is relative and, therefore, the idea of love, honesty, and truth being absolute values is sheer fiction. Moreover, the outward conduct of every cynic cannot help being a direct reproduction of his or her belief. But the new spirit which Jesus brought revolutionized life — it cleansed human attitudes, laid restraints on human conduct, and molded into new patterns the careers of human character. In all those who opened their hearts to Jesus, God worked towards the higher benefits and ends of his purpose. The eternal spirit in concert with human life produced a life of satisfaction, which was to stand everlastingly as the proof of God's integrity and power.

3. The world saw how this new spirit provides power to realize whatever it promises. The famous American editor, Horace Greeley, told of receiving a letter from a woman who wrote: "Our church is in dire financial straits. We've tried everything to keep it going: a strawberry festival, an oyster supper, a donkey party, a turkey dinner, and, finally, a box social. Will you please tells us, Dr. Greeley, how to keep a struggling church from disbanding?" Dr. Greeley wrote back to her a message in two words: *Try Christianity*!

What did he mean by that? Look at it in this way. The ancient world failed to help men and women meet the problem of life, because, although their wise men could teach, they could not supply the power to put it into practice. The Old Testament prophets could explain the Law of Moses, but were unable to provide the power needed to fulfill it. Then, into the midst of the ages, came this man Jesus and, before the wondering eyes of men and women, he declared, "I am the way, the truth, and the life." These people saw truth coming alive in his amazing personality; and, when his enemies finally killed him, his great spirit was liberated to be wherever needy souls cried out for him. In all the ages since, for all those who have received him as the bread of life by committing their lives to him, he has brought power over their every weakness, victory over every failure, and conduct and character that have made the world a better place in which to live.

One of the greatest Christian women of these past one hundred years was Lady Aberdeen who came from a Highland home in Inverness, Scotland. She lived before all the fuss and feathers of feminism and women's liberation; but, when she died in 1939, the record of her achievements read like a scroll of honor. In 1882 she founded an orphanage for Scottish children which was dedicated by Prime Minister Gladstone. In 1893 she founded the "Onward and Upward Association" to help domestics get education and recreation beyond the drudgery of their jobs. In 1897 she founded the Victorian Order of Nurses to help sick folk on the lonely Canadian frontiers. In 1919 she led a delegation to the Peace Conference in Geneva on behalf of the women of the world. Someone asked her what was the strength that undergirded her life and character so that she was able, for sixty years, to give herself to the needs of the world? Just before her death in 1939, she wrote: "I find my one resource is to throw myself in unreservedly on the power of the Holy Spirit. . . I make it a practice to stand in a certain place where I can look up at the mountains and say, 'I can do all things through Christ who strengthens me.' "

This is the same power that not only makes you and me *do* great things, but, basically, to *be* what we are; it gives quality to all we say and do. St. Paul said, "By the grace of God I am what I am." Jesus said, "The words that I have spoken to you, they are spirit and they are life." That same spirit of power is available today to all who will accept it and stand in obedience to God's will.

After this many of his disciples drew back and no longer went about with him. Jesus said to the twelve, "Do you also wish to go away?" Simon Peter answered him, "Lord, to whom shall we go? You have the words of eternal life; and we have believed, and have come to know, that you are the Holy One of God."

John 6:66-69 (RSV)

John 6:66-69

Holy Friendship

Jesus said to the twelve, "Will you also go away?" Simon Peter answered him, "Lord, to whom shall we go? You have the words of eternal life."

It is easy to think of Jesus' life as being calm and quiet, with hours of solitary meditation or periods of religious conversations with his chosen Twelve. There were such times, it is true, but scarcely a day passed without some crisis erupting over things he said and did that were different from the beliefs and lifestyle of even his own people.

Today's text signals a watershed in the progress of his witness and mission. The multitudes were waiting for him wherever he went and his popularity and success were becoming a reason for jealousy, on the part of the representatives of organized religion, and for awe and wonder, among the common people. On this occasion, some thousands had followed him around the north end of the Sea of Galilee where he taught them and, when the evening came, he fed them by multiplying a meager supply of fish and bread. Immediately a wave of enthusiasm swept over the crowd; they went crazy about him and they wanted to make him their king on the spot. This was not "in the cards" for him, and he slipped away into the mountains alone. When he returned, there they were again;

not really to get further teaching, rather they wanted more bread. But Jesus tripped them up by declaring, "Do not work for the food which perishes, but for the food which endures to eternal life." (v. 27)

That did it! They wanted bread, but he was giving them words, words, words about God and some other bread, the bread of life. When no further miracle was forthcoming, they quit, and we read, "Many of his disciples drew back and no longer went about with him." (v. 66) They wanted to make him their type of Messiah. However, Jesus' focus was not on a kingdom of this earth, but of heaven — the rule of God in the human heart. As A. S. Peake comments: "He threw cold water upon their Messianic enthusiasm and sent away from himself some who were his loudest followers." Then there were the Twelve — they too, in all likelihood, had subtle misgivings. "Will you also go away?" asked Jesus. Not plaintively, nor with a "poor me" attitude, but he spoke with a note of challenge, for immediately Peter seemed to take heart and said, "To whom shall we go? You have the words of eternal life."

Doesn't this incident sound a note of familiarity among all of us today? In the church? With its many religious organizations and agencies? Consider some of the facts. In 1985, the Presbyterian Church (USA) registered a decline of 43,000 in membership. The Roman Catholic Church anticipates the number of its diocesan priests to drop from 34,000 to 18,000 by the year 2000. Put Jesus' question to the rank and file of church members today and what will be the likely replies? We cannot understand the vocabulary of the church; all this talk about "eternal life" is beyond us. We believe in the Golden Rule, that's all; this business of faith and commitment seems unnecessary. Jesus, if he were alive, would not be "with it" today; this Kingdom of God stuff is vague and irrelevant. We take a look at the church, at the set who attend it, and none of them seems to count for anything. Look at the figure it cuts. Where is its impact? Are there really any winners there? Let

Jesus ask these folk, "Will you also go away?", and imagine how they would look on him with pity. Yet, some Peter among them may still step forward and tell the world why he and his company choose to stay. "Where else can we go?" he asks courageously. You have what we desperately need — the words of eternal life.

1. Let us look at his words. What is the significance of words anyway? Words are the medium of thought, but more important, they convey the person. And the more relevant they are, the greater the impact they have or make. The deeper need of those multitudes around Jesus was to get right with God, not necessarily material bread. And Jesus' words were directed to that human problem or situation. Moreover, his words and his person were so united that, as it was said of Rudyard Kipling, "His words became alive and walked up and down in the hearts of his hearers." Jesus' words arrested attention and held people in their grip. "No man," the people said, "ever spoke like this man." (John 7:46) "Heaven and earth will pass away, but my words shall never pass away." (Matthew 24:35) Robert Menzies commented: "His words were organically related to himself. When Jesus speaks we get himself."

So far, so good; but there was more. Jesus' words were *saving* words. They were warm, instructive, and sometimes judgmental, but always they were the vehicle of his person, one whose human concern had the spirit of a God of love in them. Hence they were reconciling words. For those who hear and accept them, "There streams into our life an energy which enables us to live in a way which our flesh and blood could never achieve." (A. S. Peake) Peter spoke truly for these disciples: in fellowship with Jesus they had come in contact with his amazing spiritual power and, listening to his words, he became for them the living center of their life.

2. Let us look at his offer. Explore the words of Jesus and one finds, running through them, an offer having to do with fuller and more meaningful life. Listen to his striking

declarations: "I came that they may have life, and have it abundantly." (John 10:10) "The bread of God is that which comes down from heaven and gives life to the world." (John 6:33) "I am the living bread which comes down from heaven . . . he who eats this bread will live forever." (6:51, 58) And, in exchange for this gift, all he asks of men and women is to believe.

Why should anyone refuse or turn away? The offer is unparalleled in the whole story of human experience, but to maintain a sustained belief is more than many of us can do. We see it in church membership. People take vows and join the fellowship of the congregation, but soon drop out. We see it with church leaders. They are called to think through the fundamental ideas of the faith; but many of them find this too demanding, and they retreat back onto *square one*. We see it with evangelistic campaigns where hundreds are carried forward with the crowd, but discover, all too readily, that Jesus makes demands upon them they cannot accept. We see it with others who were in the church by tradition, but became somehow convinced it was impotent in the face of the world's general breakdown and the ravages of the home front through violence, drugs, pornography, and dog-eat-dog lifestyles. Like these, will you and I also go away? More pointedly, should the question be put: to whom *can* we go? Is there really anyone else we want in exchange for Jesus? Can anyone suggest someone better to whom to turn?

Jesus' offer still stands after twenty centuries. And we know from those who have stayed with him, those for whom he has been the bread of life, that there is no one they've found who can give them the kind of life he offers to those who believe. David H. C. Read once said: "I have heard, as a pastor, hundreds of reasons for quitting the church, but never has anyone said to me, I'm leaving the church because I've found someone better than Christ.' "

Second Series

Questions Jesus Provokes

Now when the Pharisees gathered together to him, with some of the scribes, who had come from Jerusalem, they saw that some of his disciples ate with hands defiled, that is, unwashed. (For the Pharisees, and all the Jews, do not eat unless they wash their hands, observing the tradition of the elders; and when they come from the market place, they do not eat unless they purify themselves; and there are many other traditions which they observe, the washing of cups and pots and vessels of bronze.) And the Pharisees and the scribes asked him, "Why do your disciples not live according to the tradition of the elders, but eat with hands defiled?" And he said to them, "Well did Isaiah prophesy of you hypocrites, as it is written,

'This people honors me with their lips,
but their heart is far from me;
in vain do they worship me,
teaching as doctrines the precepts of men.'

You leave the commandment of God, and hold fast the tradition of men."

And he called the people to him again, and said to them, "Hear me, all of you, and understand: there is nothing outside a man which by going into him can defile him; but the things which come out of a man are what defile him." For from within, out of the heart of man, come evil thoughts, fornication, theft, murder, adultery, coveting, wickedness, deceit, licentiousness, envy, slander, pride, foolishness. All these evil things come from within, and they defile a man."

Mark 7:1-8, 14-15, 21-23 (RSV)

How Do You Remain Religious?

". . . and there are many other traditions which they observe. . ." (v. 4b)

The most powerful questions Jesus asked were those that made the persons being addressed raise further questions. These occasions created for him opportunities to do his best teaching. The incident Mark tells us about in our text today was just another encounter between Jesus and the scribes and Pharisees. They were always watching him and his disciples in order to find a *cause célèbre* by which to cast this new movement into an unfavorable light. They were legalists and an issue was given to them ready-made when they saw the disciples partaking of a meal without washing their hands.

"So what?" we would say today. But not so in Jesus' day. The situation was as follows: there was the Jewish Law which was basic and inviolate. But through the years the scribes and other religious thinkers wanted the Law broken down into all sorts of amendments, exceptions, and appendages, until it developed into thousands of fussy and picky regulations overseeing every possible human situation. This was known as the Tradition of the Elders and, in many cases, it exercised a stranglehold upon religious life. In this case, for example, although the Law required one to eat only with washed hands, the tradition prescribed exactly how it was to be done; the detailed procedure was nothing short of appearing ridiculous. Jesus stepped into the controversy and gave his word of judgment by quoting the prophet Isaiah: "Isaiah was right when he prophesied about you hypocrites in these words: 'These people pay me lip-service, but their heart is far from me: their worship of me is in vain, for they teach as doctrines the commandments of men.' " *(NEB)*.

Then came the follow-up. Jesus moved in on the particular situation. For him, eating with unwashed hands did not render any person unclean in the eyes of God. Nothing that enters anyone through the mouth will make that person unclean. It is only what comes out from the heart, i.e., from the moral and spiritual consciousness, that makes a person to be approved or disapproved of in the sight of God. Joseph Parker commented, "Before God, life is not a question of washed hands, but of a washed heart; it is not a question of how one kneels, but of how one prays."

In terms of life as we know it, what are the human faults and failures intimated here?

(a) These scribes and Pharisees were off-center in their understanding of what is true religion. Ceremony had become, for them, an end in itself; hence, meticulous observances of rules and regulations was, to them, service to God. As long as one recognized God's existence in a prescribed and courteous manner, one was religious. Mere churchgoing, for them, would be the stuff out of which religion is made. Outward observances were a be-all and end-all and, in so acting and believing, the question of the attitude of one's heart towards God did not come up.

(b) These critics of Jesus were at fault because they had become slaves of orthodoxy. Don't the road signs in front of some church buildings cause a scornful burst of laughter? "The Orthodox _____ Church!" Such titles reek with presumption because, like the scribes and Pharisees, these twentieth-century legalists make religion the product of their mind, and not of simply listening to and accepting the voice of God. Splitting theological hairs and slavish dotting of the "i's" and crossing the "t's" of a creed can never usurp the true essence of the Christian religion.

(c) Further, these carping critics in Jesus' day had a narrow perspective on how religion was to be practiced. Everyone must be religious in one way — their way. As long as men and women carried out their worship and obedience to the Law in a supposedly correct ritual, these persons were automatically good. What does it matter if they hate others or carry envy, bitterness, or jealousy in their hearts?

These are the attitudes and forces Jesus was up against. He bore down upon blind bondage to tradition among these supposedly religious people and what he told them was revolutionary. No wonder they hated him! But he stood firmly on the side of truth: what goes into one's body cannot defile a person. Kosher went out the window! Religion incorporates principles, not constrictive rules and regulations. Many people, then and now, were and are committed to God, but they fail in how this commitment is maintained. Moreover, this *art* of remaining religious is determined by the basic factor Christianity affirms to be the key to the good life, namely, the renewal of the human heart. This is what Jesus said to Nicodemus: "Except a man be born again he cannot see the kingdom of God." (John 3:3) There is no other way, because it is out of the heart the issues of life come, and, therefore, the roots of sin must be torn from us. Someone said, "There is no power on earth to make a bad heart good." Or, similarily, to keep it so. Social reforms cannot do it. Education cannot achieve it. Armed conflict cannot enact it. Initially, it is the human mind that makes the decision to accept Christ; but it is the heart and will that make that decision stick and keep it firmly faithful to the end of one's life. Daily commitment to his person and prayer pleading to God for strength to do it are the ways to remain religious. The mechanics of religion are secondary. A constant pledge of personal loyalty must have priority.

Then he returned from the region of Tyre, and went through Sidon to the Sea of Galilee, through the region of the Decapolis. And they brought to him a man who was deaf and had an impediment in his speech; and they besought him to lay his hand upon him. And taking him aside from the multitude privately, he put his fingers into his ears, and he spat and touched his tongue; and looking up to heaven, he sighed, and said to him, "Ephphatha," that is, "Be opened." And his ears were opened, his tongue was released, and he spoke plainly. And he charged them to tell no one; but the more he charged them, the more zealouly they proclaimed it. And they were astonished beyond measure, saying, "He has done all things well; he even makes the deaf hear and the dumb speak."

Mark 7:31-37 (RSV)

Mark 7:31-37

How Does Religious Conduct Work?

Some people brought him a man who was deaf and could hardly speak . . . Jesus took him off alone . . . looked up to heaven, gave a deep groan, and said to the man, "Open up!" . . . and he began to talk without any trouble. (TEV)

As churchgoers we talk about the worship service, but the Society of Friends has rightly cautioned us by pointing out that there is the hour of worship and at the conclusion of it, service begins. The lesson is that, in Christian living, worship and service are not merely a one-hour simultaneous exercise on Sunday morning, but service is the outgrowth of worship and worship inspires, defines, and shapes our service. Alexander Maclaren spoke aptly and well on this very matter when he said: "In our work, what we do depends largely on what we are, and what we are depends upon what we receive, and what we receive depends upon the depth and constancy of our communion with God."

Our text brings us the story of one of Jesus' early miracles. His fame was spreading and we read of crowds of both curious and needy folk pressing in upon him so much that he was not able to be alone for a moment with his disciples or himself. Mark comments, "He could not be hid." (v. 24) On this particular day, on an excursion on foot from Tyre and Sidon towards the Sea of Galilee, he was stopped by a small unidentified group who brought to him a deaf-mute, a man who couldn't hear and who had an impediment in his speech. They begged Jesus to "lay his hand on him." Jesus took him aside, apart from the crowd, "put his fingers in the man's ears, spat, and touched the man's tongue. Then he looked up to heaven, gave a deep groan, and said to the man, 'Open up!' At once the man's ears were opened, his tongue was set loose, and he began to talk without any trouble." *(TEV)*

This is the story. But in many similar cases in Jesus' ministry, usually a controversy preceded or followed the incident. Here, however, we have a simple account of a healing miracle that evoked no pros and cons, that seemed to have a routine character about it, except that the people "were astonished beyond measure." (v. 37)

Whatever may have been Mark's purpose in telling or preserving the story, one thing must be made and kept clear: this is not primarily a picture of a deaf-mute being cured; it is basically an insight into the person of Jesus. The man tells us nothing, but Jesus conveys lessons to us by what he shows us of himself. And one of the most effective pieces of instruction here is how Christian conduct works. Suppose then we examine Jesus at work.

1. "Looking up to heaven." (v. 34) This phrase tells us one thing in particular: Jesus was able to do what he did because he was a channel through which God's power was brought to bear upon a human situation. Living communion with God was the dynamic beneath the exceptional abilities people saw in his daily conduct. Preceding and within every crisis, it was this constant personal relationship to God that fortified him, and the necessity always to nourish it was among the strongest precepts he gave to his disciples.

For us, Peter T. Forsyth put the matter thoughtfully when he wrote, "Unless there is within us that which is above us, we shall soon yield to that which is around us." Yet, even among church people, this injunction is painfully neglected. We live in an era of feverish activity. Quiet fellowship with God is not eagerly sought nor easy to come by. Solitary hours and inward meditation are no longer admirable habits. We are so busy thinking, discussing, and inquiring about things secular that our timetables allow little space for us to be still. Jesus would tell us today that our souls are starved and he would invite us to "come aside and rest awhile." We have inherited all the perils of having lost vital contact with him who is able to give to our lives that extra his risen spirit makes possible for him to share. Without realizing it, our Christian disposition has lost control of our conduct, our conscience has become dulled, our sensitivities blunted, and, like Paul, we cry, "For I do not do the good I want, but the evil I do not want is what I do." (Romans 7:19) Jesus, "looking up to heaven," in the face of one of life's great demands helps us, as Samuel Miller remarked, "to find the point again."

2. "He gave a deep groan." How alien this seems to Jesus' conduct! Almost invariably we note Jesus' attitude and bearing to be filled with joy, exhilaration, and tones of victory. However certain and true this is, by his very nature, Jesus could actually groan. The dictionary defines "groan" as a noise indicating great inner strain. Jesus' heart was a well-spring of sympathy — his tears at the grave of Lazarus; his weeping over Jerusalem as the Passover drew near. His humanness: "wearied (he) sat down beside the well" (John 4:6); "he was in the stern (of the ship), asleep on the cushion." (Mark 4:38) In this way, he was one with us; but more: his groan meant he felt the heavy burden of human need. Just one deaf-mute before him, but, as Alexander Maclaren wrote: "The whole weltering sea of sorrow that moans around the world of which here (this man) is just one drop." This the scribes and Pharisees, with all their splitting of legal and theological hairs, could not see nor feel. But Jesus' lifestyle indicated that, in order to heal, one must stoop to the level of those to be healed. As someone said, "We must lower in order to lift." We do no good to cases that see

us shrink from them. (Father Damien, on the leper-infested island of Molokai, found he had to become a leper himself in order to be their helper and friend.)

To live out the Christian life sincerely and to its fullest, only a groan will indicate the depth of our concern for struggling and needy humanity. It is easy to write a check, send a *care box,* or dole out welfare packages like bones to a dog. Can we blame such recipients if they spurn us or become irritated? Our conduct must be shaped by one who said, "Learn from me; for I am gentle and lowly in heart . . ." (Matthew 11:29) In that spirit he consorted with publicans and sinners and, as Paul, his follower, said, "I have become all things to all men, that I might by all means save some." (1 Corinthians 9:22)

3. And Jesus "said to him, 'Open up!' " What was so wonderful about Jesus was his realism and activism: realism in that he faced up to the facts; and activism — he carried through in order to finish the job. His gazing into heaven and his inner groaning must have created an emotional wave among the people and, by their very human nature, they must have been asking within themselves, "What now?" Is anything going to come out of all this? Jesus knew the danger of exciting people and then letting them down anticlimactically. He refused to work on the mind and heart and exclude the will. He said to the deaf-mute, "Open up!" To quote Maclaren again, "The surest way to petrify the heart is to stimulate the feelings and then give them nothing to do." This is the story of much of the emotional religion abroad in America today. Emotional religion divorced from action results in sentimentalism, insincerity, self-adulation, and hypocrisy. Equally perilous is the desire to be liked or popular, because it tends to compromise the Gospel, to make religion comfortable, and to cater to human wishes rather than people's needs. Jesus, on the other hand, held to his own basic need: a constant link with the unseen; to deaf-mute humankind, the need to know we, as Christians, are with them in their struggle; and, for the helpless world, their need to see how God and his chosen Son share power that turns defeat into victory.

And Jesus went on with his disciples, to the villages of Caesarea Philippi; and on the way he asked his disciples, "Who do men say that I am?" And they told him, "John the Baptist; and others say, Elijah; and others one of the prophets." And he asked them, "But who do you say that I am?" Peter answered him, "You are the Christ." And he charged them to tell no one about him.

And he began to teach them that the Son of man must suffer many things, and be rejected by the elders and the chief priests and the scribes, and be killed, and after three days rise again. And he said this plainly. And Peter took him, and began to rebuke him. But turning and seeing his disciples, he rebuked Peter, and said, "Get behind me, Satan! For you are not on the side of God, but of men."

And he called to him the multitude with his disciples, and said to them, "If any man would come after me, let him deny himself and take up his cross and follow me. For whoever would save his life will lose it; and whoever loses his life for my sake and the gospel's will save it. For what does it profit a man, to gain the whole world and forfeit his life? For what can a man give in return for his life? For whoever is ashamed of me and of my words in this adulterous and sinful generation, of him will the Son of man also be ashamed, when he comes in the glory of his Father with the holy angels."

Mark 8:27-38 (RSV)

Mark 8:27-38 (C)
Mark 8:27-35 (L, RC)

Proper 19 (C)
Pentecost 17 (L)
Ordinary Time 24 (RC)

What Does Jesus Expect of Us?

"For whoever would save his life will lose it; and whoever loses his life for my sake and the gospel's will save it." (v. 35)

This event at Caesarea Philippi is regarded as a watershed in Mark's gospel and, indeed, of Jesus' ministry on earth. Here was the hinge of the *before* and *after*. All that had been said and done before this incident was preparatory to it; all that followed was colored by Peter's confession of the messiahship of Jesus. Up to now, the thrust of Jesus' message was the Kingdom; from this time onward, the focal point would be the Cross.

Prior to this event, there had been tumultuous weeks and days. Wonderful works had been performed — the hungry were fed by the thousands, the blind had sight restored, the dumb were made to speak. As a result, an emotional wave was everywhere mounting among every group — the common people, the *church* hierarchy, even the disciples. The emerging question was, "Who is this man?" The sick are cured? The winds and waves obey him? Is he just the carpenter from Nazareth, or isn't he? Then, in the quiet company of his disciples, the issue was joined when the Master turned to them and asked point blank: "Who do you think I am?" Peter — always forward Peter — replied, "You are the Christ."

Consider what this confession meant within the context of the crosscurrent of opinions in that day. With the disciples there was a consistently deepening conviction which grew from the general to the particular and was the product of their close fellowship with Jesus. Initially, they must have seen, in him, just an ideal man, a person of great humanity, a teacher with extraordinary insights and gifts, and a personality that drew people of all kinds to him. But, very soon Jesus, for them, outgrew this conception, for he seemed to possess a mysterious relation to the whole human race. His concern and helpfulness reached out to everyone and this Kingdom idea forecast a new society that would embrace all humankind. But there was much more: the longer these disciples were with him, the fuller they sensed, in his person, a presence unique beyond all ordinary experience; they felt the unseen touching their lives through him, and they might well have said, "To know him was to know God." This is what Peter brought into focus when he said, "You are the Christ."

The matter, however, does not end there. If Jesus is the Christ, the promised Savior of the human race, what follows now? What is to be expected of those who were his closest companions? And what is our task as part of the community of Christian believers today?

1. Jesus expects us to see Christianity in the light of his person. For many people today religion is no more than what they can get out of it. There is a religion of self-centeredness published from many Christian pulpits in these days, and blandished continually by televangelists over the *tube*. Its sales talk is: expand confidence in your own self and capture fame and fortune as your reward and prize. Even those who claim to be most "orthodox" err in making the fruits of religion something for one's own personal advantage. But, to qualify truly as a fellow traveler with Christ, the primary demand is to deny self. Jesus said, following on the heels of Peter's confession, "If any would come after me, let them deny self . . ." (v. 34) No one can put self at the center of his or her religion and

be a Christian, for Christianity can never be separated from him who was its founder; they are identical. The founders of other religions — Confucius, Buddha, Mohammed — might point towards truth, but only Jesus could declare, "I am the way, the truth, and the life." Those who shared in his company and the fellowship of his spirit discovered, in him, truth alive and, when they accepted it, they found, through him, the only way to live.

2. Jesus expects us to carry his lifestyle into our own calling. One of the unique characteristics of Jesus' lifestyle was the investing of his life into the training of the twelve disciples. The impact of his mission depended upon their catching his vision and kindling in them a similar enthusiasm. This was to be the seed of the church, namely, a person such as Peter catching the vision and confessing Jesus as Lord. Wherever this was done sincerely, self was obliterated and the Lord of life became the focus of the disciples' commitment and devotion. Moreover, this attitude and resolve would be the foe of self-interest. Self-sacrifice would replace any attempt to grasp one's own advantage.

In this, Jesus' expectations ran counter to the selfish interests of the power structures of his day and wrote the ticket for his eventual doom. "Deny self . . . lose life for my sake and the gospel's" — what do we have here anyway? The chief priests were bent upon saving their own positions and fringe benefits. The Pharisees did not care a hoot for the poor and outcast, but were concerned with legalistic details to save their own hides. The Zealots wanted to knife Rome and return to the ancestral power of the days of yore and, hence, they spurned any notion of a spiritual kingdom.

All these factors and factions were eating at the heart of the nation. Jesus felt the necessity, for the sake of his own people, to live out to the fullest the only lifestyle that could reform and save the human spirit and be an everlasting example before the world. "He who would save his life shall lose it . . . For what does it profit a man, to gain the whole world and forfeit his life?'' (v. 36) And this he expects of everyone still.

Happily and fortunately, again and again in the story of the Christian faith, countless ministers and missionaries of the Cross have been caught up with the grandeur of this sacrificial enterprise. Denying comforts, careers, and material gain, they have said, with St. Paul, ''Henceforth let no man trouble me; for I bear on my body the marks of Jesus.'' (Galatians 6:17)

3. Jesus expects us, by sharing his life, to reach an understanding of what our life ought to be. William Barclay wrote, ''God gave us life to spend and not to keep.'' There are life hoarders whose eyes are always on personal comfort, worldly status, and financial security. They build around themselves walls of protection to keep every challenge and trouble out. Theirs is a prescription for stagnation. They are unaware that, in spite of their caution, they are actually losing the life they have. But if they were to turn away from their protective security and let their lives, talents, and assets loose into the world of human need, they would accrue dividends of self-fulfillment, personal enrichment, and inner satisfaction nothing else can give.

Today, in the world of science, space, medicine, etc., there is a galaxy of experts who take risks, work to exhaustion, and live on the edge of burnout, because they seem to know where to put their values in life. All of them seem urged to pioneer against the tremendous odds of disease, poverty, and human ignorance of this universe. Daily they say ''No'' to every temptation to give up, to quit. Something within them compels them to go on, to stay on, and to out-think the mysteries of his far-flung world.

And what of Christianity and the servants of its faith? Jesus still says: ''He who would save his life shall lose it; and whoever loses his life for my sake and the gospel's will save it.'' Do we have in the world of the Christian faith the same investment of ''time, talents, all,'' as among the analysts, inventors, and researchers of the secular realm? Jesus constrains us to gain that sense of purpose which comes through commitment to what God wants for his world. We can learn it from Jesus as we see him leave Caesarea Philippi and carry his mission to Calvary. T. R. Glover said, "God could do no better than to be like Christ." From him we get a clear notion of the purpose for which we were born and, with it, we receive the vision and resources to carry it out.

William H. Foulkes makes us sing:

Take thou ourselves, O Lord, heart, mind, and will;
Through our surrendered souls thy plans fulfill.
We yield ourselves to thee — time, talents, all;
We hear, and henceforth heed, thy sovereign call.

They went on from there and passed through Galilee. And he would not have any one know it; for he was teaching his disciples, saying to them, "The Son of man will be delivered into the hands of men, and they will kill him; and when he is killed, after three days he will rise." But they did not understand the saying, and they were afraid to ask him.

And they came to Capernaum; and when he was in the house he asked them, "What were you discussing on the way?" But they were silent; for on the way they had discussed with one another who was the greatest. And he sat down and called the twelve; and he said to them, "If any one would be first, he must be last of all and servant of all." And he took a child, and put him in the midst of them; and taking him in his arms, he said to them, "Whoever receives one such child in my name receives me; and whoever receives me, receives not me but him who sent me."

Mark 9:30-37 (RSV)

Mark 9:30-37

Are Greatness and Christianity Compatible?

On the way they had discussed with one another who was the greatest . . . And he [Jesus] took a child, and put him in the midst of them . . ." (v. 34, 36)

In Shakespeare's *Twelfth Night*, Malvolio comments: "Some are born great, some achieve greatness, and some have greatness thrust upon them." There is a large measure of truth in this observation, but it falls short in any discussion of greatness from the Christian point of view. True greatness is neither born in you, nor achieved by you, nor imposed upon you. It is caught, for it is the byproduct of the deeper qualities of our human nature.

Our text is from a tiny, yet significant, vignette from the course of Jesus' ministry, particularly related to his instruction of his disciples. On an itinerant mission to Capernaum, Jesus overheard the disciples carrying on a rather heady and stealthy discussion of their own. When they arrived at the house (presumably Peter's), he asked them what was the subject of their *tete-a-tete* out on the highway. Obviously they were somewhat ashamed of themselves, for they met Jesus' question with an embarrassed silence. Apparently Jesus suspected what had been the thrust of their clandestine debate and he broke the silence with this apt comment: "If any one would be first, he must be last of all and servant of all." (v. 35) Then, Mark reports, "He took a child [maybe one of Peter's children], and put him in the midst of them." Amiel, the nineteenth-century Swiss philosopher, once commented: "Blessed be childhood; it brings down something of heaven into the midst of our rough earthliness."

The issue here was not that the desire for greatness could be sinful in the eyes of God, but concerned something more basic — ambition. This was the underlying and ruling passion with this coterie of disciples. Ambition, however, can be neutral. It is good or bad depending upon what a person is ambitious for and why. Being ambitious for greatness for one's own or for greatness' sake can be destructive of the best within us and of our usefulness to others. Often, as William Barclay said, ambition is, for some, a matter of "How can I shine?" rather than "How can I serve?" Jesus took the concepts of "ambition" and "greatness" and put them into the framework of human conduct, and showed how this ambition to serve alone produces a type of greatness that claims our enthusiasm and contributes mightily to the common good.

We read: "He took a child and put him in the midst of them." How simple a gesture! Yet, often Jesus did this kind of thing. In so doing, he moved a critical matter from the realm of theory and into a living situation: he brought in a person. Remember many other and similar occasions when he did the same: "A certain man had two sons . . ." "A man was going down from Jerusalem to Jericho . . ." "The land of a certain rich man brought forth plentifully . . ." Imagine the effect of putting an innocent little child in the midst of these querulous disciples! What would they see in a child? Plenty: no sifting of qualifications in an effort to be top banana; no struggle to name and rate one's own abilities; no score card listing of personal merits; no top-level plateau from which to lord it over others.

Instead, the child portrayed humility and did so unconsciously, an innocent freshness remote from well-worn arguments of these rustic men, and no hangover of guilt from things said and done in regretful yesterdays. Likely these disciples became aware of what Canon Elliott meant when he said, "There is always something lost in growing up." Jesus (to quote Elliott further) "was calling upon these disciples to cherish and to keep if they could the childlike spirit and the childlike heart, the childlike way of looking at life, the childlike way of believing in life, the childlike way of waiting confidently for what life has to bring." To live with a childlike spirit will temper our every ambition and cleanse them from narrow concern for self. Chiefly, however, in conformity with Jesus' teaching and example, Christians will allow themselves to be absorbed into the community of a kingdom where no one fights to be first and where greatness is the legacy of each person who volunteers to be servant of all.

Now, what must we grown-ups resolve to be and to do in order to respond positively when Jesus puts a little child in our midst?

1. We must recapture the sense of wonder. Ours is a materialistic age. Only what can be seen and handled visibly seems to count. Only what is spelled out in black and white is believed. "The world is too much with us," as Wordsworth wrote. We have lost our horizons. The horizon is where the heavens meet the earth. "Trailing clouds of glory" reads silly in these secular times. Such is dubbed as passé. Life is devoid of the element of surprise. Where is the world of wonder of the little child? True, there is the element of naiveté in juvenile wide-eyed wonder, but in our quenching it within ourselves, we have almost destroyed beauty with our ugly graffiti, allowed utility to design our buildings, and not gracefulness, and permitted cold facts to create an era of speed. Wonder has gone out of our music and, hence, it no longer soars but trudges in a monotonous beat. Wonder has slipped from our painting and without the "sky" we get senseless daubs of colors.

Wonder has left our literature and, instead of great imaginative novels, we are given only the seamy side of life.

Jesus "took a child and put him in the midst of them." This was his way of showing men and women there was another dimension to life than they had ever recognized. Parables, miracles, teaching made them see that life was not merely a-b-c, that there was a world of the unseen impinging upon their ordinary commonplace living and, if they opened their hearts to it, they would see, as James S. Stewart said, "wonder upon wonder and every wonder true." The dimensions of true greatness do not lie in our world of gadgets and things, of push and shove, by which our ego is expanded, but in that scheme of wonder where self-denial makes lesser people great.

2. We must cultivate openness of belief. Nothing is more detrimental to genuine Christianity than the closed mind. It appears in the fundamentalist who stands rigidly upon the verbal accuracy and inerrancy of the Bible, in the Roman Catholic deification of its own ecclesiastical system, and in the legalists who, as Jesus commented, "strain out a gnat and swallow a camel." (Matthew 23:24) The result is not one kingdom under Christ, but a whole miscellany of defensive kingdoms, each condemning the other for its heretical or offbeat position. Jesus faced a similar hodgepodge in his day; he saw people and movements stultified by human isolationism and separatism. All of it pointed to the tragedy of the closed mind. Again and again he laid his finger upon human attitudes as "the villain of the piece." Little wonder the presence of the little child both judged and enlightened those whose closed minds repudiated the nature and method of Christ's kingdom.

What a difference the childlike attitude and spirit work in the affairs of the kingdom! The child represents openness, a readiness to receive guidance, instruction, and gifts, and in simple trust which accepts without thinking that he or she must now add up the totals in order to be sure to pay God off. Jesus taught that the kingdom of God was offered and given to all who were open to receive it and, unless they accept it without stipulations and conditions, (like little children), they are not eligible to receive it at all.

There is one thing more. Receiving the kingdom does not depend only upon our attitude of openness and humility; something further is there — the possibility of growth into spiritual maturity, to become the persons God wants you and me to be. Christ has set the standard for us and his offer is still valid: "Behold, I stand at the door and knock; if any one hears my voice and opens the door, I will come in . . ." (Revelation 3:20) True greatness is standing near. Need we ask how to come by it?

John said to him, "Teacher, we saw a man casting out demons in your name, and we forbade him, because he was not following us." But Jesus said, "Do not forbid him; for no one who does a mighty work in my name will be able soon after to speak evil of me. For he that is not against us is for us. For truly, I say to you, whoever gives you a cup of water to drink because you bear the name of Christ, will by no means lose his reward.

"Whoever causes one of these little ones who believe in me to sin, it would be better for him if a great millstone were hung round his neck and he were thrown into the sea. And if your hand causes you to sin, cut it off; it is better for you to enter life maimed than with two hands to go to hell, to the unquenchable fire. And if your foot causes you to sin, cut it off; it is better for you to enter life lame than with two feet to be thrown into hell. And if your eye causes you to sin, pluck it out; it is better for you to enter the kindom of God with one eye than with two eyes to be thrown into hell, where their worm does not die, and the fire is not quenched. For every one will be salted with fire. Salt is good; but if the salt has lost its saltness, how will you season it? Have salt in yourselves, and be at peace with one another."

Mark 9:38-50 (RSV)

Mark 9:38-50 (C, L)
Mark 9:38-43, 45, 47-48 (RC)

Proper 21 (C)
Pentecost 19 (L)
Ordinary Time 26 (RC)

When Is It Tolerable to Be Intolerant?

"No one who performs a miracle in my name will be able soon afterward to say evil things about me. For whoever is not against us is for us." (vv. 39, 40, TEV)

Two words in our vocabulary conjure up opposite types of persons: the tolerant and the intolerant. One seems to wear a white hat; the other, a black one. Two little verses set these types in clear contrast. Jonathan Swift wrote:

We are God's chosen few,
All others will be damned;
There is no place in heaven for you,
We can't have heaven crammed.

Edwin Markham wrote:

He drew a circle that shut me out —
Rebel, heretic, thing to flout.
But Love and I had the wit to win—
We drew a circle that took him in.

These two attitudes underlie this passage in Mark's Gospel. Here we note three groups of sayings of Jesus, each of which suggests either the presence or absence of tolerance.

I

First of all (vv. 38-40), we have Jesus' disciple, John, coming
to him and raising a complaint. John and his brother, James,
were sons of Zebedee and were nicknamed "Sons of Thun-
der," because they were somewhat precipitous in their actions
and judgments. What upset John this time was the sight of
a man, who was not a member of the disciples' group, exor-
cising a demon from another man and doing so in the name
of Jesus. The belief current at that time was that "if one could
get to know the name of a still more powerful spirit, and then
command the evil demon in that name to come out of a person, the demon was supposed to be powerless to resist." (William Barclay) Jesus' response to John was a cryptic remark:
"He that is not against us is for us." This settled the case of
John's intolerance.

And so with us. Intolerance stalks our footsteps whenever,
in life's affairs, we condemn people who do not do everything
our way. For example, take our Christian worship in all its
multiple forms and practices. Don't we still have, in our
churches, people who say to their neighbor, "You worship God
in your way, but I'll worship him in *his*"? Intolerance scowls
and says there is only one way to God — *mine*! Others have
no right to their own thinking. "It's a fearful thing," writes
Dr. Barclay, "for any man or any church to think that he or
it has a monopoly on salvation." And G. Johnstone Jeffrey
commented, "See that you do not deny the name of Christian to another because he or she is not wearing your label,
denominational, ecclesiastical, or theological." Christian tolerance invites us to sit down together and assess our beliefs and
doctrines by the kind of people they produce, by what these
do for human need, and how limited really are our little ideas
in the face of Christian truth. Bare intolerance has no place
in Christian thinking for, as Dr. Barclay commented further,
"Every man in need has a claim upon us because every man
is dear to Christ."

II

Second (vv. 43-48), Jesus indicates the dangers that lie in tolerance, in *laissez-faire*, in indifference to things as they are regardless of their obvious insufficiency. Always Jesus set before his disciples the greatest goal of all, namely, life; and for him that meant being in the Kingdom of God. What was meant by the kingdom? Simply this: wherever God's will was recognized and done. In his prayer given to the disciples, the petition reads, "Thy will be done on earth as it is in heaven." Now this is not attained by our own wisdom, talents, or powers. It is received as a by-product of faith, commitment, and complete surrender. But this does not mean we can remain inactive, nor is it suggested that we can tolerate allowing our spiritual capacities to continue in a half-developed state. Discipline, self-denial, and sacrifice are meant to prevent any organ, spiritual or bodily, getting in the way of our goal. We are not to tolerate the do-nothingness of lazy tolerance. G. K. Chesterton reminded us, "Merely having an open mind is nothing." All of us must stand for something or else we shall fall for anything. Ours must be a discriminating tolerance.

III

Third (vv. 49, 50), Jesus talks metaphorically and uses, as his idiom, salt, an element very familiar to his people because of the role it played in their whole culture and economy. The idea here is that there needs to be an intolerance of tolerance. And the character and activity of salt illustrate aptly what Jesus meant. The Christian life is not all softness, relaxation, and "me-too-ism." There must be salt in it, for salt, like fire, has a purifying function. Moreover, it brings out inherent flavor and preserves what might otherwise decay. For us, in daily life, G. J. Jeffrey wrote about salt, "There must be something in it comparable to the stinging saltness of the sea-breeze, smarting, stimulating, giving tone to our whole system."

Here is implied, moreover, that for you and me to be truly Christian we must have strong convictions about what we believe and about how we act and why. They must not be wishy-washy and tolerant of all fuzzy opinions and attitudes. Jesus said, "Have salt in yourselves, and be at peace with one another." This is the happy combination of an informed intolerance and a balanced tolerance. An open mind is a tolerant one, but it cannot tolerate that which prevents us from becoming and continuing in what life in God's kingdom requires. "Sooner or later," wrote Ned Rorem, "you've heard all your best friends have to say. Then comes the tolerance of real love."

And Pharisees came up and in order to test him asked, "Is it lawful for a man to divorce his wife?" He answered them, "What did Moses command you?" They said, "Moses allowed a man to write a certificate of divorce, and to put her away." But Jesus said to them, "For your hardness of heart he wrote you this commandment . But from the beginning of creation, 'God made them male and female.' 'For this reason a man shall leave his father and mother and be joined to his wife, and the two shall become one flesh.' So they are no longer two but one flesh. What therefore God has joined together, let not man put asunder."

And in the house the disciples asked him again about this matter. And he said to them, "Whoever divorces his wife and marries another, commits adultery against her; and if she divorces her husband and marries another, she commits adultery."

And they were bringing children to him, that he might touch them; and the disciples rebuked them. But when Jesus saw it he was indignant, and said to them, "Let the children come to me, do not hinder them; for to such belongs the kingdom of God. Truly, I say to you, whoever does not receive the kingdom of God like a child shall not enter it." And he took them in his arms and blessed them, laying his hands upon them.

Mark 10:2-16 (RSV)

Mark 10:2-16

Proper 22 (C)
Pentecost 20 (L)
Ordinary Time 27 (RC)

How Can We Restore the Christian Home?

And they were bringing children to him, that he might touch them; and the disciples rebuked them. But when Jesus saw it he was indignant, and said to them, "Let the children come to me, do not hinder them; for to such belongs the kingdom of God . . ." And he took them in his arms and blessed them, laying his hands upon them." (vv. 13, 14)

The Christian home, once the stable element in the structure of our Western society, is besieged today from without and within. Without is an age of bloated agendas, hurried and frantic claims upon our time and resources, to such a degree that the average American home has no identification except as a crossroads where its family members encounter each other on their way to somewhere else. Within is a rumpus room where there are no longer any shared interests and goals, no coming together of the aspirations of human hearts and wills, and where each family member is an isolated unit without communal support. Sad, isn't it? But glaringly true! And we have ample evidence to support the inevitable and disastrous results. (One or two up-to-date national or local domestic crises may be cited here as examples.)

Take a moment to reflect upon what in America we now have: one marriage in three ends in divorce or separation; the number of "latch-key" children, the offspring of single parents is alarmingly on the increase; the helterskelter of much contemporary home life leaves teenagers to follow the line of least resistance on their own; tragedies occur with such shocking impact that forces many parents to face each other wonderingly and ask, "What did we do wrong?"; our daily newspapers give us pause when we read (cite either facts or some statistics from one's local situation).

In view of all these negative and distressing facts, how very much beside the mark seems to be the question: "How can we restore the Christian home?" The prior question, however, is "Do we want to?" Not the strictly puritanical and patriarchal home of the New England of a century or so ago or the unbearable modern fiction of the Falwells, Helmses, Hatches, and Swaggerts of our present time. It must be granted, however, that some such homes produced a great man or woman, although it is not clear or provable that their greatness may have emerged in spite of their environment. And there are other exceptions: someone was the product of a broken home and, by some grace, rose above it. Nevertheless, the facts of history, past and present, present us with a more or less preliminary question: what should we work towards, as far as the contemporary home is concerned? We have tried many remedies, but these have merely taught us that we cannot patch up a mess. Maybe the Gospel of the New Testament has something to tell us, if only we could take time to read and listen. Let us come to Jesus where we find him in Perea, a sort of scrubby bush country area of Palestine, and where the people, especially the women, spent their lives in a twilight of hope. They had little to which to look forward, yet they apparently had a deep concern for their children; and hearing of the presence of this "stranger of Galilee," they brought them to him — an action quite alien to their rustic and superstitious traditions about the caring for and handling of children. Note, however, the adverse reaction of the disciples at the intrusion of these women; note the verbs "rebuke" and "hinder." They might have said, "Clear these little monsters out of here!" But Jesus was "indignant" and he upset their prohibitions and said, "Let the children come to me, and do not hinder them; for to such belongs the kingdom of God . . . And he took them in his arms and blessed them, laying hands upon them." What a juxtaposition of human attitudes and sentiments, of the negative and positive, we have here: the disciples' "rebuke" versus Jesus' "indignant"; the disciples' "hinder them" versus Jesus' "let them come to me"; "whoever does not receive the kingdom as a little child" versus "he took them in his arms and blessed them."

What has this incident to tell us that might be helpful to the question before us? Can we restore or maintain the Christian home today? Yes, we can, but it can only be done if we take some essentials of our faith and put them to work in the critical situations of our times.

1. We must understand the real meaning of family responsibility. This brings us to the very essence of the Sacrament of Baptism. Herein, however, lies one of the greater sins of omission of our church. Many parents are not informed of or taught what the baptismal ceremony means and entails. Some think of it as something similar to an injection; the baby must be "done," as if it were a sort of sacred vaccine. Others treat it like a social event, a family get-together in which champagne á la the launching of a ship takes precedence over the symbolism of the water. Or, some others treat it as an act of dedication in which what is done is entirely on and from the human side, and what God has done, does, and will do is not taken into any account. All these notions are spurious and they circumvent the responsibility factor at the heart of it all.

This brings us to the key word, "covenant," which defines for us the connotation of responsibility in the context of the Christian life. A Christian covenant involves not just two persons or parties, but three: father, mother, and God. With two persons only, it is just a pact like any secular agreement. But a covenant involves far more: it is a sworn agreement to which God is witness and in which God's concept of sincerity, justice, and faithfulness is the standard by which to live. What an awful sense of responsibility this implies for us! Note, for example, the verb in verse 13: these women were "bringing" their children. They didn't "send" them as many parents do with their children, either to Sunday school or to church. They came themselves, taking their children with them. In other words, they brought their home to the church. And our responsibility incorporates much of the same. With the whole family coming together to Christian worship, there is involved here a commitment and witness to the good life that re-forms the ideal family, Sunday after Sunday, as a unit within the kingdom of God's will and peace.

2. We must cultivate those basic spiritual factors necessary to creating sincere personal relationships. Douglas Goldring, the English novelist, in his book *Nobody Knows*, has one of the women say this:

"It's all wrong, Gilbert. I just hate this new-fangled nonsense about marriage being hell and women being slaves and all that. Of course it's hell and I'll tell you why. It's hell because of three things which are common to both sexes: selfishness, ill-temper, and bad manners. They're all curable; but the divorce court won't cure them; it never has and it never will. Love's a thing that grows slowly and has roots and can stand wind and weather."

Centuries ago, Tertullian wrote: "How beautiful, then, is the marriage of two Christians, two who are one in hope, one in desire, one in the way of life they follow, and one in the religion they practise."

Both of these opinions are true. Only a vital religion can provide the power needed to cultivate and sustain this love that cements human relationships in depth and through time. You see: all love is of God, and all hatred and enmity are of the evil one. Since God himself is love, then true affection in the home is more likely to deepen and endure where his presence is acknowledged, honored, and made central. Where love is, God is. And the home where such a reality is cherished will be a fruitful soil for the growth of mutual love, honesty, and respect.

The Christian home, however, is not an end in itself. There is a creativity in Christian love. If it is genuine, there is a continuity that goes on and on. When our children go out into the world to make their own homes, what will they most remember? If they have seen goodness in their parents' home, they will not be likely to doubt or scorn it in their own. If they have experienced estrangement, aching hearts, and long silences dispelled by repentance and forgiveness, they will know that love can flow back in through the window out of which it had flown. They will know that when trust has been broken, it can always be claimed back. But most of all, they will testify that pride, egotism, and orneriness are a sacrifice which precludes the sacrifice of the home.

Jesus, through the power of his Spirit, is able to renew and restore the many good and great things which somehow we have lost. The disciples, by their staid opinions and resentments, symbolized an old and wornout world. Jesus made the world young again as he took the children into his arms and blessed them. He put new life into the idea of a kingdom. He can bring the same to every home where there are people who believe in him, love him, and take him in to live with them.